Living in Phases

Living in Phases

Leisly Ann Roman

ALEGRIA
PUBLISHING

davina@alegriamagazine.com

Número de Control de la Biblioteca del Congreso: 2023905078

ISBN: 9798986084497

Publicado por Alegria Publishing

Portada y maquetación del libro: Carlos Mendoza

Dedication

This debut poetry collection is dedicated to:

Every creative who has yet to share their art
/ believe in themselves – please do not deprive yourself
of the difference you can make, if not to another,
than to your own self.
You're just as important as the others,
and your art matters just the same.

-

Mi mami, who for years upon years has
repeatedly professed two things to me:

1. *"Leisly, you need to write a book."*

2. *"La vida no es una papaya."*

Maybe one day I'll finally figure out
what in the world she means by the latter.

-

Me.
I'm proud of you.

Table of Contents:

Preface

"I am going to make something of this pain. I am going to highlight every 'little' win. I am going to write this into my future."

Literally.

As a little Leisly, books were everything to me. In elementary school mi mami would greet me the moment I arrived home and, on some days (the best days), would send me straight to my room for a surprise. On my bed would lie a brand new book - from popup picture books to a title from the "Chicken Soup for the Soul" series - crisp pages and an unbent spine induced feelings of joy and anticipation that little else could bring about so rapidly in my fragile little self. Fast forward a decade later, and words still mean quite a bit to me. English became my favorite class in school, essays and discussion boards were always preferable to multiple choice exams and dreaded oral presentations - I found a comfort and, more importantly, a confidence in words, that I would struggle to find anywhere else for years to come. That to be honest, *I still struggle to feel today.*

In 2017, arguably one of the most difficult years of my life, *I sought therapy for the first time. I unboxed, uncovered, unloaded, so much.* This was also the year I was officially and finally diagnosed with Obsessive-Compulsive Disorder. I argued with my psychiatrist you know - told him he was wrong. I was clearly depressed. Anxiety and intrusive thinking were mere disturbances that were obviously clouding the actual problem. He responded with a slight smile and quickly asserted that I had "won the lottery of mental illness" with my diagnosis (more on that later, for sure). I cried. I journaled about it. I ate and starved and slept my shame and frustration away until it became clear that I was only getting worse. More out of control, assuming that I ever was in it. Work was disheartening, my studies were exhausting, and I had developed what felt like a paralyzing belief that I was nearing a dead-end, both professionally, and academically. *What disappointment Leisly Ann, what is your papi going to say? What chismes will your tios and tias say about you over the phone? How will you ever measure up to your little sister? Did tu mami really sacrifice it all to raise you, to fail?*

2021. New place of work. New school. New degree. *"Why do I still feel this way, why won't my mind just give me a break?" "Por Dios que tengo que hacer para sentirme normal?"* This is when I found poetry again. In the span of a few years I had experienced more grief and exhaustion and guilt and embarrassment and confusion *at the hands of my very own body, of my very own mind,* than any soul on this Earth should be subjected to. *How do we escape ourselves? How do we escape the desire to escape ourselves?* By this time though, I had also healed parts of me I truly didn't know even needed to be. I changed, and I like to think it was for the better. I owe much of this change to my first therapist, much of it to myself, and much of it to poetry. I cannot really say what brought me back to poetry, but I can say, *so much of what this collection represents - resilience, growth, vulnerability, bravery - would not have been possible for me without it.* "Living in Phases" is a poetry collection primarily focusing on mental health, and written for those currently in a difficult, painful phase in their life. It is also for those who are making strides to change their situation, manifest the future they desire, and become the kind of person they know in their heart they want to be. Finally, it is a collection for those who are in the process of healing - from anyone, anything, or any moment. Life is a series of phases, and like the moon, we exist in these phases. That's just it though, *we continue to exist*. The pieces in this book are offered to you humbly from the soul and the mind of a hurting, and healing poet. I hope you find yourself in some of these words, and I hope that they remind you that wherever you are in life, is not where you'll always be. That is okay though, because perhaps the next phase, will be everything you need it to be.

From my heart to your hands, and with so much gratitude.

- L.A.

Para
(Mami)

¿Y qué sera de mi
si no te tuviera a ti?

un mundo total
y totalmente grande –
es fácil sentirse pequeño

pero a tu lado he crecido
aprendido,
a conocer lo grande en mí;
nunca más
me olvidaré
yo nací para ser grande también

Nothing is easy. Everything, is hard.
Nada es facíl. Todo, es difícil.

another day, another trigger / what's the plural for
"another?" / the word seems rather inaccurate / or
maybe it is not, since "another" implies "singular," and
frankly I can't seem to complete one singular task
without spiraling out of control / an entire evening and
the morning thereafter engaged in a one-on-self debate
/ the topic of question: will I skip tomorrow morning?
— spoiler alert: I skipped / the result: my mood is low,
but my pride is high / don't tell me it's a delusion. I am
tragically self-aware / except now I cannot determine
if I did it for the sake of my mental health, or my
physical health / perhaps neither? / perhaps just another
condition of my illness(es) / perhaps even, even just a
little bit, for the sake of this poem, and its credibility-
my credibility / who's to say / perhaps for now I'll just
confess to you how I ended this morning's journal entry
/ excuse my all-or-nothing thinking / perhaps it's just
another intrusive thought / or maybe, I just might be
onto something /

nothing is easy. everything, is hard.

The problem with me
is that I can't seem to learn
a new way to be

Perhaps the simplest way to frame it
is without a frame at all
for I am but a photograph
with no place up on the wall–
I haven't the aesthetic of black–and–white images
or the authenticity of photos creased
colored with histories exuding enchantment
details worth remembering, to say the least–
And so was born the fear
I've feared for far too long–
that I'll always be the photograph
that just does not belong

they say your body is your home
I'm afraid I've been an awful housekeeper-
the seeds of my mind only sprout plants of anxieties
and bouquets of fears
it's no wonder this garden
hasn't grown anything beautiful in years

they say your body is your home
I'm afraid I am an awful housekeeper-
tell me, do you think this, too?
I tried my best to water your favorite ones
even if it meant drowning in you

they say your body is your home
I'm afraid I'll always be an awful housekeeper-
if I ever come alive again, in another time, in another life
please plant my seedlings at the nearest beach
let the corrupted ones dissolve instantly in the sand
let me know a life without this mental strife

how easy it is to get lost in a mind
that feels wholly
and utterly
blank

how?

there are no streets
to take a wrong turn on
no hills obstructing my view,
my mind houses no sidewalks
with confusing signage-
"Kids at Play" and "Yield"
are no concerns of mine-

my mind is blank, things should be clear;
clarity, I fear, is far from near

I'd like to see the world
more clear
and speak to souls a bit more
sincere

who have no intention
of leading me astray
leaving me suspicious
of the words they say

to learn life's truths from books
and passed down tales
rather than heartache
from avoidable fails

oh, I yearn to see the world
more clear
for I've grown tired
of living in fear

I feel at times, that
my hope will guide my journey-
Is this, why I weep?

I've found that it
is much too easy
to submerge into one's own mental sea
to be swallowed by incoming waves
of thoughts
you thought
you'd left behind;
Past experiences
of dread, of bliss
color your mind chaotically
then disappear in the open water
as a new tide settles in.
This one different than the last
yet equally destructive,
turning moments
not yet had
into feelings of fear
and despair
that arise almost as naturally
as the Sun, peeking out across the sea.
A new day, yet again.
Will I be thrust backwards,
lunged forward?
I contemplate this daily.
All the while also wondering
why I find it not as easy
to submerge myself in the present.

and I'll give this page
one quick, soft tear
before I allow
my thoughts to share
with you
or frankly, anyone
what lies deep within the depths
of a soul shielded from the Sun;

the days turn to weeks
the weeks, to months
where light does not shine
and so therefore the hunt
for purpose, for meaning
for feeling begins
a desperate attempt
before the darkness wins–
again

It's never enough–
The twists, taps, touches and tears;
Please mind, please, *not now*

you think me well-
dramatic, even perhaps-
to say that I am afflicted
by the insidious grasp of addiction;
because a scale cannot compare to narcotics
nor a mirror, to a bottle of Brandy
you look at me and think me to be
perhaps,
out of my mind
all the while blinded
oblivious
to the simple truth-

I was starving

of nutrients
of rest
of reasons or energy or will
to defend myself against my own spirit-
the greatest adversary I've ever faced-

but mostly
I was starving for hope-
a hope
that has been off the table
for likely
far too long

isn't it funny how we grow
out of things

skip. resist. restrict.
I used to envision being a vision from behind now I'd give
anything for the need for a belt

patterned dress pants and jumpsuits from 3 Christmases ago
I save them
and together they create quite a requiem for the past;

even in front of the mirror
I see a second me
and ironically, this is where I'm most often reminded,
I am facing my demons alone;

let me trade you this pullover-*it's really quite cozy-*
for that two-piece you wore on vacation last summer-
you won't miss it, I swear, people like you have to spare-
come on a simple body swap is
    all
       I'm
          asking
             for

no
for once I want to grow
in

in love with the parts of me
that give away neglected traits of my
identity-

yes, these are my real curls,
you know these hips are no size two but they may be too
much to handle
for you–
and in acceptance of all
that has helped me build
the one I am becoming–
what made me think she wasn't the same one I've been
forever tearing down?

isn't it funny how naturally we grow out
of things
and how forcefully we must grow in–
to, ourselves

there's a dampness in the air
that grows with every passing hour
intensifying
tightening
it's grasp upon the present
subtly reminding me,
of every crippling moment of solitude
I've ever felt before
of every jarring realization
of isolation
that's ever settled within my bones;
I walk along a backdrop
of opaque greys and dull whites
I see no light on the horizon
showers, must still be passing through

ask me what is precious to me
I will say
my education
ask me what has caused me grief
I will claim
my education

early years of my life spent
on mastering basic arithmetic–
future decades of my life spent
counting calories, cups and spoonfuls–
did I ace that science quiz in high school
covering principles of volume and mass
only to torment myself years later
meticulously calculating
the space this body of mine holds
in a room
in a dress
in the life of an acquaintance or loved one?

No.
Or perhaps, yes?

my life, blessed with education
for this I know to be true
my mind, cursed with knowledge;
I am at a crossroads, and know not what to do

at times I feel
many things all at once
sometimes I feel nothing
but hopelessness;
the absence of negatives
I've learned
does not necessarily manifest
the presence of positives
in *emotion*
in *spirit*
in *life*

and in the end I am ripped apart
by a bittersweet sense of pride
by a clash of emotions
painfully impossible to hide

a sense of pride looking back
at the days you consumed me
compared with days of the present
and of a mind who's since then been freed

only to find myself
riddled with fear and despair
as I consider your mind
and how long it's been since I held a place there;

it is a cruel and painful irony
the act of moving on
while for me, a work in progress, I still hurt
at the thought of me being long gone

to you

"Old Friend"

What good do you serve me?
Beneath my feet
Yet above my head
What a foul trick I'll not ever comprehend

By taking 2 steps forward
I take 20 steps back
(at least)
I convince myself the satisfaction will be worth more
than some unnecessary feast

Then I proceed to compare
        Compare
                Compare
                        Compare
Oh look, who knew rock bottom had a basement

Though I'm no stranger to the dark –
I like its silence, please, don't join me -
To bear the weight of these thoughts,
sometimes my body pays the cost

"An Ode to What I Never Asked For"

a bit of deceit,
irrational fears nestled in
deep-
a standard thought is made up of these

a piercing disguise
to shield my
demise
now I hide behind walls and not masks

erected solely from the fear
a simple mask
can't contain tears-
at least not in the way that cement can

now I'm alone in a home
that sends sorrow
through my bones-

how I wish I had built something kinder

My anxiety often mirrors
a natural disaster, an earthquake
destroying everything in its path,
crippling me from within.
And as the ground opens up beneath me
as environmental turmoil sets in
emotional debris surrounds me;
intrusive thoughts destroy the very foundation
that took too long to construct.
And as the ground opens up beneath me
I wonder, *will I survive this time?*
As I have so many other times–
or so I thought
foolishly.
And as the ground opens up beneath me
I feel myself sinking *lower, deeper.*

My anxiety often mirrors
a natural disaster
an earthquake
destroying everything in its path,
crippling me, from within.

The most recent chapters
of my story
weigh heavy on my heart.
The pages are damp,
the tone is somber–
a reflection of my longing for you.
The words,
once a source of relief
now appear awfully blurred before my eyes–
my eyesight,
once clear,
now only focused on my search for you;
Though I know where you are,
the coordinates won't suffice–
I'll need more than a lifetime or two
to recover the remnants
of what's left of my hope–
a consequence of my quest for you.

"Stuck"

Too heavy have become my feet
to travel the distance ahead
for it seems as if it's been too long
since the path was paved, and led,
to any imaginable destination
that would obliterate the source
of my current distress and anguish
and place me on a newfound course

But when reality strikes,
it strikes hard and it seems cruel;
I am reminded of what I am without-
a compass, a guide, map or tool
to weather what must be confronted
in order to find my way;
how I yearn to have the courage
to make it out of here someday

and in the end
if I had known
the mark you'd make-
or rather, leave behind-
if I could have imagined
the moments I'd create
deep within my mind
knowing full well
my imagination
was as close as I'd ever get
if someone had warned me
of the sleepless nights ahead
and the times I would convince myself
I'd feel this way
for good

believe me,
if I had known,
I would have still said hello

if only a heart
were as easy to mend
as a broken or fractured limb
for I cannot think
of any adhesive
with the capacity to repair
the tears in what once was
      or what could have been
           or might have been
if potential had not clashed with timing,
to blur the line between affection and lust
and with this blurred line
a troubling thought comes to mind-
the hardest kind
of heart to mend
is the heart that has broken itself

Loneliness
is the enemy of transparency;
to share my thoughts, but be misunderstood
state my point of view
and feel the crush of rejection–
no, I do not want to be alone
with my thoughts and fears
a 10-ton weight–
what I crave is to be safe;

Loneliness
sometimes feels just the same

"That's so OCD!"
my peers exclaim
as I mourn the loss of control,
and they feign the loss of it

a stereotypical portrayal of my illness
                    is inadequate
                    at best
a stereotypical portrayal of my illness
                    is disastrous
                    at worst

I needn't look out
my windows to know the Sun
has set I feel it;
outside the world is quiet.
sigh. inside's too loud to bear.

it's been awhile
since I've dreamt
dreamt of anything really

maybe because
it's been awhile
since I slept soundly, through the night

at peace;

peace

I took for granted as a child
a child who never once
dreamt of a world
where nights and peace
did not coexist

settled in bed
just past midnight–
I hear my neighbor's fence outside
engaged in a vicious battle;
the wind seems to be winning

the weight of my body
upon my right side
my head,
just at the edge of the bed
so heavy with thoughts
I fear it might roll off

settled in bed
just past midnight–
the wind has quieted down
now if only my mind
would do the same

"I Seek Relief"

I seek relief
from an overactive mind –
she tells me to hurry then herself, slows me down,
I wear her coercion like an adorned, embedded crown –
from an overworked body –
it is exhausting, you see, to force myself to tend
to me, through relentless compulsions I'll not ever comprehend –
manipulated by fear.
When the self becomes irrational,
incomprehensible, to say the least,
then free will, a mere illusion
and logic, too far from reach.
And I worry
that my arms
will never suffice.

"The Wind"

It carries away my secrets
my most troubling fears
my most threatening thoughts
like a mail courier-
I offer up a package,
no return address in sight;
It's chilly outside,
It's loud inside.
I listen, as it blows through the trees —
the leaves don't stand a chance
and in that moment, I understand
how they might feel, if only they could.
For I know what it is
to fall victim to forces
seemingly more powerful
than ever you will be;
I listen
as someone else's demons are thrust against my window
and my package
it joins theirs, and so many others.
Oh, wind-
I hope you travel far tonight.

tell me why
in every tongue I speak
I am only fluent
                    fluida
                            fluente
in painful promises
and self-given grief

out

of will / of skill / of my daily evening pill - / *the pharmacy closes up shop at 9PM but I've long stopped believing they stock what is needed to mend* / this ache - / of reasons at the moment to try / or fight / or turn on the light - / "*¡¿Cómo tú vez en esta oscuridad?!*" / *mami,* / *the darkness blankets what the light painfully illuminates* / *can you not tell I am just trying to survive? -* / of time, perhaps / though I may have decided that on my own / it's just hard to forsake / *the seeds of deficiency I've sown*

everything
every single little thing
I do
is wrong;

I shut my drawers with a force I know is not innate to me,
as I stand and straighten
their wood morphs, it curves
through silent splinters I hear them mocking me
wrong;

and what a shame I did not sweat or move or *live* enough
today–
my clothes don't reek of city hustle and bustle
they are not stained by rebellious remnants
of the day's affairs
that refuse to be forgotten
they are clean
mi papi pays too much in bills as it is
so I suspend my top with felt
my bottoms with plastic
and my visions of normalcy
with the remaining strings of my faith
and shut the door–
will / did / can my fingers cover enough square footage
of those hangers?
wrong;

my lips are dry in complete contrast
to my pupils–
drenched with despair
dripping droplets of hopelessness–
I seek relief from the dark blue chapstick atop my bureau–

with SPF, the good kind-
I settle for grief as I snap back on the cap
you guessed it
wrong;

before I allow the night to end
retire this body, descend
into subconscious stories and unconscious peace
I ritualistically band together
index, middle, and ring-
right hand only, no exceptions-
and place
on my statue of the Virgin Mary
who watches over me every night-
is this inappropriate? did I touch the right spot? twice is
unspeakable but did you consider perhaps thrice?
wrong;

one, two, three, uno, dos, tres, do, rey, me, "Hail Mary...,"
"Our Father...," "Hello Lord...,"

I cannot talk or study or musically lift
or pray my way out of this one
I've tried
and it's not that I lack faith
or even what it takes
it's just, in this moment, I am cocooned-
meticulously woven
protectively constructed
I cannot escape, because I am not meant to
I cannot escape, ~~and I don't know if I want to~~
this is who I am.

her illness
made her intransigent-
she was unwilling to bend

all or nothing, black or *white*
into dark thoughts, she'd descend

only to re-emerge
a bit more broken,
a bit less hopeful, *that there'd be an end*

tell me
how does one renounce the pain
they've sealed within their heart –
in every piece
of its shattered remains?

stuck–

or maybe just in slow motion
at a constant yellow light;
I want nothing more
than to *accelerate-*

either way I'm
at a loss
for words
motivation
inspiration

it's so hard to forge
what cannot be forced

I live in fear
that my emotions will spill out of me;
my body a glass
overflowing with liquid
~~flooding engulfing~~ *drowning* all in its path

the mess left behind
will be mine alone to bear

"Quiero Entender..."

my first psychiatrist told me
I'd won the lottery of mental illness-
"Idiota" thought I. luck was far
from on my side

my very first therapist
Dios la bendiga, she moved mountains
on the terrain that is my brain-
did you know there could be flowers despite heavy,
relentless rain?

recently my current specialist
with soft and gentle eyes
asked me if I felt okay-
I think she knew what I would say-
and what I said was something along the lines of
"Absolutely not"
in other words
that is to say
"quiero entender mi manera de ser"

I've lived one too many years-
scratch that, call them what they are,
lifetimes
under a cloud of inner strife
it's closest companions, two twin lightning bolts
that cut hope like a knife
for sport
for karma
or perhaps for the simple purpose of *having purpose;*
aun así no sé por qué esta tormenta llega siempre

"Tell Me, Do You?"

do you miss me;
the faint smell of my perfume
that lingered behind for a moment or two
like a trespasser in your space?

do you hear me;
the sound of firm boots passing by
with subtle heels
that kept us at constant eye-level?

do you feel me;
when the warmth of the morning's sunrise
touches your skin
and the peace of the evening's sunset graces your soul
granting you encouragement- as I always did- to unwind
and let go?

"do you miss me?"
"do you hear me?"
"do you feel me?"
"are you capable of... any of it?"
I've asked myself this time and time again
only to be confronted
with an even more incessant thought-
I miss you, I hear you, I feel you,
as I exist here and now
today.
I am incapable of otherwise.

"The Cruelest of Tricks"

convince myself into submission
time and time again
treat you as the opposite of what you truly are
surrendering willingly to, a "friend"

each time it hurts a fraction more
than I could've ever imagined
the numbness starts to fade away,
I'm left frustrated, and *saddened*

I note it's been this way for years now
does that mean anything at all?
I've learned that human beings are meant to rise
and undoubtedly to fall

in love, in line, in holes *too deep to climb from*
no matter the length of the ladder or rope-
and I was meant to succumb to the cruelest of tricks
of the mind, for a *semblance of hope*

If time in fact
does heal all
then all clocks around me
must have come to a stall

For I've known little peace
since the night I had learned
that your feelings, perceptions
in another direction had turned

And though piercing to me
inclined I am still to say
I pray you are better than me
at finding your way

over a decade later
I'm still trying to find my way
lost in the body they built
anchored down by these feelings of guilt;

one
  two
    three
      four
step

what will you say today old friend,
I've been awfully meticulous–
have I made them proud this week?
they'll say otherwise, but I know,
it's the right number, that they
seek

this pain is suffocating / but not in the way you might
think - / see, I have enough air / in fact, / I have
enough to spare - / it's all-encompassing / and what it
encompasses / is *toxic;* / fighting fumes of impending
failure / fanning flames of forsaken hopes - / they
say recovery isn't linear / *(true)* / though don't always
mention / it's not really much easier / to attempt to
climb a crooked rope ; / this pain suffocating but I'm
not afraid / of losing air - / I'm afraid I simply won't be
me / if I ever learn / to breathe without it

Ojos, color cocoa,
piel, color miel,
cada uno de ellos perfectamente posicionados,
para ver cada parte de ti que has dejado
perder

Ojos, color cocoa,
piel, color miel,
desde niña te dijeron "flacuchenta,"
y ahora las libras extras son las que más puedes
ver

Ojos, color cocoa,
piel, color miel,
llevamos veintiséis años juntos,
dime:

¿Cuántas decadas más para tener
tu ~~aprobación~~ amor?

If not me, then who?
Si no yo, entonces ¿quién?

If not me, then who?
I ask myself, what needs to
change?
Needs to stop?
Be reframed?
I ~~ask~~ remind myself
Si no yo, ¿entonces quién?

"The Time to Rise Has Not Yet Gone"

Though the Sun has set
A flower still will bloom, and
You, a bud, will too

I am but a cloud;
Though I may appear still,
I am always moving

Carried not by the winds of a jet stream
No, but by moments, by beliefs,
By experiences;

The smallest of droplets
Create the most massive
Of clouds

I am learning to view my progress
My growth
In perhaps a similar light–

seemingly meaningless
yet,
ultimately ever-powerful

to turn cognizance
into action
in the interest of self-respect
is an art I've not yet mastered–
as the sole creator
of my life
in this life
it is my responsibility
to demand nothing less

I live in shades of black
and white

> *I've yet to outgrow my own hypocrisy,*
> *my own contradictory*
> *~~nature~~*
> *(how terrifying it is to think that this was my fate,*
> *that there is no cure)*

I thrive on order, I'm convinced doctors only know
how to make a fuss
their MRI machines display a brain that lights up,
gleams with chaos-
my mind's garden may be filled with wilted roses,
untilled soil
and seeds that sprout only the kinds of weeds
that'd cause the most compassionate beings to recoil

> but I have hope,- *I know, some audacity-*
> that somehow, someway,
> the days ahead are colored in hues of *free;*
> mellifluous affirmations sprout to combat
> somber thoughts,
> a blessed existence no longer plagued by constant
> relentless fraught-

> *perhaps one day*
> *I'll finally learn to see gray*

Free.
I want to be free from
a mind that which I cannot control
and a body that which I cannot nurture.

Free.
From the belief that which
was ingrained in me long ago
claiming that I was a wilted flower
in a world,
no, garden,
no, field
of bouquets.

Free.
From the constraints of the buttons on my pants-
shackles, that keep me from escaping
this prison I've created within.
No visitors allowed.

Free.
To break free;
to break loose.
For I hold the key
to the shackles that hold me.

it took
a transition
from looking outward, to focusing inward
to ~~realize~~ take accountability for once and for all
that it was not my special circumstances
that fostered grief in me;
it was what I chose
to allow
to be

the most breathtaking waves
are often a product
of the strongest currents

on land this still holds true-

resilience
is not innate,
and it is only found
in the most breathtaking of humans
often up
against the strongest of currents

I say a prayer
every morning
or night
with the hope that a higher power
will lend me His ears, will hear;
I am not ashamed to plead
bear no self-pity, as I beg
for the world is far too filled
with false prophets,
harbingers of discouragement;
for a future with everlasting uncertainty
needs a present held together with hope
and so I say a prayer
every morning
or night
with the hope that a higher power
will lend me His ears, will hear
and I pray
to always
be heard

"Tiene que venir de ti."

that's what mi mami always says
except now I hear it in a different sense–
the sense that this life
is mine
to bend

my feet shake atop unsteady rocks
I say to myself, *"hold on"*

reach the top of a mountain
only to find myself
at the bottom of a waterfall
where the water rages miles below
at an unknown speed, to an unknown destination
disturbing not one of these rocks on its journey
for unsteady as they may be
they hold their ground, and hold it firmly
vowing not to be swept away;

no matter life's unknown disturbances,
I vowed the same that day

there have been times
brief moments in my life
where I fantasized
even desired
to be torn apart
and disregarded
like an apologetic letter
from a past lover

I do not wish to hurt
I do not long for sleepless nights
or restless days

no

I yearn for a cause
to remind myself
I am capable
of piecing myself back together
and starting anew

pain and
fear and
hurt,
alone.

how often you've felt
these debilitating sensations
is how often you've overcome
what sought to overcome you–

is how often you've prevailed.
is how often you've survived.

I am learning how to trust
in ways I never dared to before;
I am learning how to confide
in forces that I cannot see;
I am learning how to grow
exactly where I have been planted
instead of wishing I was a seed
of another kind
in a garden
other than my own

"I Will Not Abide"

Read. Write. Cry. Rest.
No one seems to know the best
way for me to heal
as if ultimately the "answer" is just not real.

I carry on–
I project as strong
while inside a mere three-pound weight slowly crushes me;
I want to flee
can you not see
how difficult it is to be,
a victim of my own cruel mind?

No, how could you know
how I feel inside
how this invisible illness
pushes me to hide
from my very own mind, knowing full well I will abide
by its rules, its tricks–
or so it thinks.

I am not my thoughts;
My compulsions are but a
nuisance- *I will fight*
So in time my yesterdays
Will know better tomorrows

The importance of protecting
your energy
your peace
cannot be overstated
and it cannot be underestimated

I don't think it always possible
to be forgiving, to be kind
to feel anything but strong contempt
for my own abusive mind–
rest assured I know I must persevere
I must do what must be done
if my destination is where I am meant to be
the journey there need only be overcome

1 step forward
3 steps back
any efforts to *"replace and reframe"*
the things that I lack
are almost futile
and in the strongest sense
I am left with the need
to recompense
those who've truly believed
that I would grow
into someone I would be proud
to know;

though I am far from this milestone
far from this feat
I've no choice but to hold on
until the day self-love, and I meet

when I look back,
back at all the times
I've allowed myself
to minimize
my very own feelings
out of guilt, or shame
I feel, not perplexed
because I know I am to blame
yet through introspection
during this innermost plight
I have learned that the only way out
is to fight
and though it may be lifelong
this battle, this war
in terms of respect
I owe myself more.

As a young girl I
tried everyday
to be loved by my family, my classmates, my friends
all the while blind
to the path I was creating
where the end destination lay a decade or so away

As a young woman I
try every day
to be loved by myself

from the depths of my inner being
I aim to fight-
until I no longer
encumber
my own self,
until I no longer
seek refuge
in reassurance,
until I no longer
bear the mentality
of a hopeless wanderer
in my very own life

and through it all I am learning
never to underestimate
the power of a strong foundation
for my skin may be thin
but my bones
are far
from frail

Every day that I
resist
Every day that I
persist
is a day I risk it all—
place a dangerous wager
that instead of I,
an anxious mind will fall

when you decide upon
a love language
make sure that you yourself
are fluent

I never was one
To know
Patience;
Forbearance- a nuisance on my journey I found to be
quite persistent-
Was never a strength I dared to claim

Until now

I will work towards
A stronger self in this sense
For this journey will be long, and tiring
And nothing short
Than worth the wait

my life
began to change
the moment I committed to believing
that dark times
can illuminate my path
and that the uncertainty I received
from myself
from others
from you
would only elucidate
that which I truly deserve
that which I truly
am meant for

One cannot stomp fiercely
on the ground
expecting flowers to bloom,
nor can they call on the Sun
in the middle of the night
begging, pleading, to escape
their fear of the dark;
should a mother bird shove
her baby bird
out of the nest t

o

o soon,
she would likely know grief,
much sooner than a mother's pride;
force cannot take the place
of patience
for patience breeds hope
and hope, *breeds peace*

"Mi Voz"

Try to silence me
You can't- poderosas son
Mi voz, mi pasión

it is difficult for me, sometimes,
to draw the line between self-love
and self-destruction;

my body pays the price, time and time again;

rest- burdensome and blissful,
are my efforts a representation
of fear of failure
disguised as determination?
of fear of illuminating
flaws not yet overcome?

I do not wish to shine this way
no; I only wish
to love without destruction

In this phase, we heal.
En esta fase, nos sanamos.

I make an effort not to seek the relief of old friends
anymore
as I know that their weight
weighs too heavy
on my soul

I only seek peace, self-compassion healthy restraint
I only seek the ways
in which
with my own heart
I make amends

the Sun will pierce your skin
and blind your eyes
and remind you that despite it all
you are here
alive

the Moon will change its shape
transform
even glow
illuminating paths on which you will allow yourself
to go

when they ask you what has changed
when they wonder what sparked the embers
you say,
"In this phase, we heal."
"En esta fase, nos sanamos."

You are entitled
to take up space, no matter
how crowded the room

"How Do You Self-Love?"

It is the healing that is felt
as droplets of water dampen the skin
under a warm shower
relieving pain in the body, the mind, the soul.
As well as the stillness that is created
as a result of conscious breathing-
mindful meditation
to soothe the thoughts for just one moment.
These thoughts may bring distress
but fear not, they cannot last
for with a journal and a pen
you can end their perceived control-
transform thoughts into words, words into sentences,
sentences into peace;
To indulge in the foods that make your insides sing
with notes as beautiful
as the smile that you generate
when you decide you deserve to be gifted.
To allow for an extra hour of sleep, or two
and arise with time to water the plants,
finish the book,
tidy the space,
complete the task that makes you feel
worthy, productive, accomplished.
Yet through all this,
this happiness,
this gift,
one truth comes to light-
oh, how selfish it is to self-love
and how lovely it is to be selfish.

"Unapologetically Alive"

Fertile soil
Watered seeds
A plentiful garden
Is made up of these

The flowers that sprout,
And move with such grace
Well, they bring uniqueness
And love to this place

And they take up space
Though they do so proudly
May not make much noise
But existing quite loudly

Existing.
Defining.
Growing.
Inspiring.

And so, amidst all the noise
lies my one hope for you–
in times of low spirits
see yourself as, a flower, too

"Let It Not Be 'You Vs. Me,' Let It Be 'Us'"

the morning Sun rises
and shines through the day
until the Moon and her stars
arrive to cast the light away

though the Moon and her stars
they do not act out of hate
not of grief, nor of vengeance
for in the shadows, they await

allow the Sun to gleam its brightest
a source of light and life for all
and when the evening hours strike,
allowing it to gently fall

I see the Sun, the Moon and her stars in us
I see them in you, and me
in order to protect our light
we must rest, find the balance, allow ourselves to simply
be

thunder consumed my city today
not a drop of rain in sight
reminding me that storms
can exist without all of their parts–
parts we've come to know them by,
and that I too
can exist without the ~~parts of me~~ anxieties
that do not
will not
cannot
serve me any longer

"Enough"

Perhaps my greatest endeavor
has been to be seen as enough.
Perhaps my greatest barrier
was not defining
what it meant to be enough.
It comes as no surprise, then,
that perhaps my greatest struggle
was understanding *I already was*.

dress yourself in clothing
as if it is intended to fit snugly around your soul
rather than
your thighs and underarms
and watch–
watch-
as the colors of your wardrobe
and spirit
expand
illuminating beauty
that already existed
but was too ashamed
to step out into the light

"Gleam"

You are the brightest
Star in your own night sky- shine
As you were meant to

I wish to be as versatile
As my favorite color- purple;
She is soft and gentle, as lavender
She is strong and extroverted, as violet;
As indigo she is dark and mysterious
Yet exudes youth and comfort as lilac;
I wish to have as many layers
As my favorite color- purple,
I yearn for the freedom to exist in many forms
Yet still be loved, all the same

"Have Patience with Yourself"

There is no right time
to be who or where you'd like
Grow at your own pace

I have learned the value
Of sincere communication;
I have dedicated time
To the practice of speaking my truth–
I will not let you equate these with being *"too loud"*

I have harnessed values
I hope will guide me day-to-day;
I have opinions,
I've taken stances–
Such a shame your stance paints me to be *"too passionate"*

No longer will I apologize
For being *"too much"*
Of anything–
For I'd rather be too much for you
Than not enough for myself

Heal
Not for the promise of a better
Tomorrow
But for the savoring of a granted
Today

to dwell on the past
is to sabotage the future
and to lay waste to the present itself

even on
and especially on
the most unproductive of days
look inward
gently
and with compassion
for uninterrupted productivity
is as painfully unattainable
as uninterrupted recovery

-keep going.

be kind to yourself
today, tomorrow
but mostly on the days your heart
is overcome with sorrow
be gentle with yourself
grant your soul a warm embrace
allow yourself to pass through this moment
with patience and with grace
be forgiving with yourself
for you are doing the best you can
making strides along a journey
only you can understand

I deserve more
than surreptitious healing,
more than fragments of sympathy and patience
from you;
I have *nothing* to be ashamed of

look upwards towards the sky
observe the clouds-
notice how they move at a pace
almost unbearably
arguably embarrassingly
slow

but the clouds they do so much,
don't they?

offer coverage from a scorching Sun
relief for parched gardens filled,
filled with sustenance and blooms-
even sometimes gathering in rather
picturesque formations
providing any onlooker
a moment of natural wonder;
the clouds above have never rushed
not once since the beginning of time
never faltered from their duties
to themselves or to us all

haste is no solution
it is the enemy of progress
time becomes less daunting
when we elect to live amongst the clouds
knowing in time, in *due time,*
we will get to where we need to go

I am practicing forgiveness
in all phases of this journey
I am cultivating gardens
dónde las semillas se siembran suavemente;

seeds of healing
to bloom with orgullo
for who I once was
for who I have become

Disposable.
Made to feel invisible
a girl who's much too gullible
and ultimately forgettable.
Am I so easy to throw away?
Is it too big a request to ask you to stay?
Reality now seems regrettable, because I
am not
disposable.

a butterfly hovered elegantly
over a cluster of brightly-colored flowers,
her wings, an eggshell white;
she flew with grace
flew with intent
flew with no dismay
for she knew
in due time
her eggshell white-colored wings
delicate as they may appear
would facilitate her journey
for as long as it would take

please don't be fooled
misunderstand
if I share with you how,
how I crave to feel your hand
in mine
for I am not disillusioned
to know the odds were not in my favor;
moments so genuine they filled my heart with gratitude
I'll hold onto, and save for later

I was fortunate to have met you
I am fortunate to have known you

Take up space
take up all the space you need

For there exists no one
like yourself
who will ever have
the same effect
who will ever shine
an equally iridescent light

Take up space
the room, will thank you

"Know My Worth"

I find it almost surreal
the challenge it is to heal
since those who've dimmed my light
gave way to tears that lengthened the nights

Prove yourself.
Improve yourself.
Do what it takes to fix yourself
or else you just won't do.

defend myself
compose myself
consistently betray myself
by breaking down my boundaries
to be replaced by walls of pain

walls of pain that,
eventually,
I found I did not care for
except for the fact
that the pain brought me insight
and inspired a drive
for something more than this

Soon I would be the one
who in the end, they'd find they miss.

to become your own muse
is one of the purest acts
of self-love.
for, to act as your own muse
is to acknowledge that you,
yes you,
are but a work of art
more powerful than one thousand words,
more valuable than any nation's currency;
it is not your responsibility
to bend to fit into the frames that others
have mounted onto their walls,
but rather a privilege, you see
to show the beauty of your canvas
unforgivingly
to all.

When the ones you thought
would stand by your side
are the ones who've learned
how to push you aside,
forgive

When the pain you thought
you had left behind
creeps up to color your world
in dark hues,
feel

When indecisiveness, uncertainty, and anxiety attack
a mind and heart at war
against
better judgement,
follow

Forgive those who have let you down.
Feel your feelings, the human experience.
Follow your intuition, wear it proudly as it guides you.
Forgive.
Feel.
Follow.
And soon enough, *freedom*.

do not be afraid
to put yourself out there
into a dangerous world of unknowns;

for all that there is, and all that there will be
cannot ever compare
to all that you are
and all that you can become

I do not want to live a life
with no regrets,
for I have been hardened through hardships
many times
and in many ways
and softened by the humility
that comes with realizing
I am human

and if the sky's hue
can change-each day, still lovely-
why not, then, can't mine?

one might argue a heart
is as complex
as the emotions that gain life within its beats;
for it truly is a tragic
yet awe-inspiring truth
how a heart that stops likely will not start again
and yet
a heart that shatters can go on
to feel more whole
than it ever had before

and in a desperate attempt at normalcy
I allowed my healing to become
the most clandestine thing about me;
try to scan our bathroom's medicine cabinet,
for remnants of my efforts
in vain–
for the Prozac, the Zoloft
lived tucked away, in a desk drawer,
behind a closed bedroom door
far from ignorant eyes;
it would be years before I at last realized
my healing
was worthy of being *known*

I am like the Moon;
I exist in phases.
Tonight, incomplete,
flawed,
a work in progress.
Tomorrow, I take on
a new shape
and shatter what was
to make room for what is to be;
for I have learned
that self-growth
often mirrors
inconsistency.

cross my path
or cross my mind
you may even cross me off the list–

but you will never
cross my boundaries
again

now I let the Sun
bleed
through my worn out window shades
her rays illuminating droplets of *hope* the Moon
left behind for me to find;
with repose no longer the enemy
light
becomes far less daunting
and a soul can learn to *flourish*,
no longer drawn to *mourn or fray;*
I shone a light on
clemency
and as a result, it only darkened my shadow –
a reminder I am not the things that I have left behind

and now he / she / they
contend – *"I will allow myself to shine."*
resplendent
restorative
resilient in body and mind
and to me it's a beautiful thing
the way we unlearn generations of darkness
the way we learn to coexist
to thrive
amongst the healing and the mess

I took the pen in hand one day / and whispered, / *"I am writing my own story."* / I opened wounds and bled on pages / and hung them up – / *made a decorative tapestry of my despair -* / then I took those pages and color–coded them – / *shades of grief, resilience, hope -* / examined every single hue / the way I imagine painters do / before they commit / *to exposing the true colors of their soul* / and then I bound them together – / *sheets filled with written candor -* / and compiled a manuscript to bare it all ; / now for the rest of my days / others will know all the ways / *this poet made it through phase after phase*

Gracias
(Papi)

Pienso que te crees fuerte
por las manos que tienes;
grandes...
o quizá, por los platos que cargas
cada día
calientes, pesados, delicados,
o tal vez te crees fuerte
por tu capacidad
de trabajar, y trabajar, y trabajar.

No.

Para mí, eres fuerte
por las veces
que tus manos
grandes
fueron usadas
para secar las lágrimas
que cayeron
una a una,
noche tras noche.

Para mí, se necesita una fuerza
para cargar
a una familia,
en una tierra nueva
que jamás ayudará
a cargar
cien platos
calientes
o no.

Y para mí
ser buen trabajador
no hace que una persona
sea fuerte;
la fuerza que tu muestras
creció en ti,
y nadie
te lo puede
quitar.

Gratitude

Thank you to mi mami (se llama Hellen), to mi papi (se llama Andres Osiris), and to my hermanita hermanita hermanita (she goes by a lot of names, but in an effort to be a kind big sister, I'll just share her legal name with you all – Giselle). Thank you for believing in me, for encouraging me, for inspiring me, *for helping to make me who I am today*. A special thanks to mi mami who always thought my writing was special. A special thanks to mi papi for accepting absolutely nothing but my absolute best and serving as a walking, breathing, living representation of what unconditional love and hard work can ultimately amount to. A special thanks to my little sister and self-proclaimed "Serotonin" for her feedback and her realness and her support towards this creation of mine. *Te quiero mucho mi gente.*

Thank you to my first therapist who gave me the space to cry and panic and, more importantly, to heal. For showing me how much I am capable of. For insisting I owed myself more. *I miss you dearly, and I hope you're doing well. I forgive you for leaving, though you don't need my forgiveness. I see now, you knew what was best all along. I will always, be indebted to you.*

Thank you to my closest friends – my travel/concert/ car ride buddy, my chosen Dominican sister, my book-loving/DIY/most inspiring and favorite educator – you all bring so much love and light and inspiration into my life. I've cried to you, grown up with you, disclosed some of the most painful parts of my existence and flipped the switch to turn the light on in some of the darkest corners of my mind without a shred of fear of judgement. I cannot possibly thank you enough. I could not possibly praise you enough. *I do not know how to possibly emphasize enough, how truly blessed I am, to be a part of your lives.*

Thank you to the online writing community who from the very beginning, has welcomed me with virtual open arms. I have never received such an abundance of support, interest, and true appreciation for my words than I have from the souls across the world I've had the privilege of crossing paths with through social media. *I will never not be grateful for your reminder that words can bring people together. I am so thankful, that they brought me to you.*

Finally, thank you to my mentor Davina Ferreira. I cannot say enough about the sheer gift this woman is to poetry, to Latinx creatives, to our community as a whole. Thank you for helping to make this book and so many other books and dreams and manifestations come true, and for dedicating so much of your time and love and energy to us all. Thank you to my Alegría familia for the feedback and the insight and the love they offered me throughout the last year as I worked on this collection, and a special thank you to Jesenia Chávez and Jessica Diaz who inspired me to take a chance on myself. *This collection would not exist without any of you. The Leisly Ann that wrote it, likely would not either.*

With my entire fragile little heart, thank you.

Prompts

It's safe to say that I would be remiss to not express
my immense gratitude to just a few of the writers and
poets I've connected with through the online poetry
community These individuals have gifted me not only
the opportunity to read their words, but with inspiration
I may have never gained elsewhere. Some of my most
vulnerable, personal, or even favorite lines or pieces were
completed with the help of prompts provided by these
incredible souls, and I cannot thank them enough for
helping me to articulate moments ranging from bliss to
strife, in a way that led me to feel a sense of catharsis,
relief, and *pride*. Below are a few Instagram handles of
writers and poets who've inspired some of the pieces
you read in this collection. Please visit their pages. Please
look at their art. Please see them as examples: *you never
know who you may inspire.*

garden body swap	@letsescapril
even if it meant drowning in you dissolve in the sand	@solaste.ame
a requiem for the past facing my demons alone	@fragmentspoetry
a color, a kind of flower, the word "free"	@disorderedpoctry
lost in the body they built	@elenaspoetry
seeds of healing	@tidesofawriter
painful promises	@alexandra.j.vincent
I am writing my own story...	@davifalegria

About

Leisly Ann is a Dominican-American writer and poet. Born and raised in New York City, and the eldest daughter of Dominican-immigrant parents, she has spent years immersed in the cultures of different lands, and has seen and experienced firsthand its effects. She is a proud member of the Latinx community as well as a passionate advocate for mental health, as can be seen in much of her writing. Living with a diagnosis of Obsessive Compulsive Disorder and plagued by what is now a decade-long battle with disordered eating, she strives to use poetry to make space for topics such as cultural expectations, self-doubt, mental illness, trauma, resilience and healing.

In 2018 she obtained a Bachelor's Degree in Psychology from CUNY Hunter College, double minoring in Sociology and Legal Studies. She then went on and earned a Master's Degree in 2020 in Forensic Psychology from CUNY John Jay College of Criminal Justice. Currently she works alongside prosecutors in New York City, assisting individuals involved in the criminal justice system with a history of mental illness or substance abuse better themselves, their lives, and in turn their communities, by connecting them to adequate programs, resources and supports. Despite her current vocation she has had a passion for writing since her youngest and earliest years. From submitting original pieces to her local newspaper for publication, to participating in storytelling contests in school, the world of literature and language has always been nothing short of fascinating, captivating, and, more so in recent years, cathartic. In her free time, you can (and most likely will) find Leisly reading another book from her ever-growing TBR list, exploring new cities and cultures through travel, binge-watching documentaries on Netflix, or immersing herself in nature. She currently resides in New York City with her mami, papi, hermanita, and sweet puppy Sky. You can connect with Leisly on Instagram at @_literaryhope, home for more original poetry and musings from the mind (and soul) of L.A.

A number of Leisly's published pieces can also be read for free in various online literary magazines such as *"The Beautiful Space," "Breadfruit Magazine,"* and *"Poetic Reveries."*